PRINCEWILL LAGANG

Wealth Beyond Boundaries: Mukesh Ambani's Rise as a Global Business Tycoon

First published by PRINCEWILL LAGANG 2023

Copyright © 2023 by Princewill Lagang

All rights reserved. No part of this publication may be reproduced, stored or transmitted in any form or by any means, electronic, mechanical, photocopying, recording, scanning, or otherwise without written permission from the publisher. It is illegal to copy this book, post it to a website, or distribute it by any other means without permission.

Princewill Lagang asserts the moral right to be identified as the author of this work.

First edition

This book was professionally typeset on Reedsy.
Find out more at reedsy.com

Contents

1 A Vision Takes Root — 1
2 Architect of Progress: Mukesh Ambani's Leadership Philosophy — 4
3 Digital Dominion: Mukesh Ambani's Technological Triumph — 7
4 Energy Metamorphosis: Mukesh Ambani's Sustainable Vision — 10
5 Navigating Challenges: Mukesh Ambani's Resilience in the... — 13
6 Legacy Beyond Profit: Mukesh Ambani's Philanthropy and... — 16
7 Future Horizons: Mukesh Ambani's Vision for Tomorrow — 19
8 Mukesh Ambani's Leadership Lessons: Insights for Aspiring... — 22
9 Mukesh Ambani's Enduring Legacy: Shaping the Future... — 25
10 Reflections on Mukesh Ambani's Impact: A Global Perspective — 28
11 Mukesh Ambani's Continued Journey: Navigating New Frontiers — 31
12 Mukesh Ambani's Enduring Impact: A Legacy of Leadership — 34
13 Summary — 37

1

A Vision Takes Root

The dawn of the 21st century witnessed a seismic shift in the global economic landscape, marked by the emergence of visionary leaders who transcended borders, redefining the very essence of success. Among these titans of industry, none shone brighter than Mukesh Ambani, a name synonymous with innovation, ambition, and the relentless pursuit of wealth beyond boundaries.

1.1 Genesis of Ambition

Mukesh Ambani's journey into the echelons of global business supremacy was not a tale of overnight success but a saga rooted in a family legacy of entrepreneurship. Born on April 19, 1957, into the illustrious Ambani family in Yemen, Mukesh inherited the seeds of ambition from his father, the legendary Dhirubhai Ambani. Dhirubhai's audacious foray into the textile and petrochemical industries laid the foundation for what would become one of the most powerful conglomerates in the world - Reliance Industries.

1.2 Nurturing Innovation

The chapter delves into Mukesh's formative years, exploring his early exposure to the intricacies of business and his relentless pursuit of knowledge. His educational journey at Stanford University in the United States marked the beginning of an insatiable appetite for innovation and technology, which would later become a hallmark of his leadership style.

1.3 The Reliance Resurgence

As Mukesh Ambani returned to India, the Reliance conglomerate was at a crossroads. The narrative unfolds the challenges and triumphs as he took the reins of the family business, steering it through a period of radical transformation. The strategic decision to diversify into telecommunications, refining, and retail showcased Mukesh's acumen for spotting opportunities in uncharted territories.

1.4 Breaking Barriers: The Telecom Revolution

The chapter explores the groundbreaking entry into the telecommunications sector with the launch of Jio. Mukesh Ambani's audacious gamble on providing affordable, high-speed internet services to the masses disrupted the industry, reshaping the digital landscape of India. The intricate details of the Jio phenomenon - from the initial skepticism to its unprecedented success - paint a vivid picture of Ambani's ability to challenge conventional norms.

1.5 A Global Vision

Mukesh Ambani's ascent was not confined to the borders of India. This section delves into his forays into international markets, strategic partnerships, and the relentless pursuit of global relevance. The acquisition of overseas assets, collaborations with international tech giants, and the establishment of a global footprint underscore Ambani's determination to position Reliance Industries as a formidable player on the world stage.

1.6 The Blueprint Unveiled

Chapter 1 concludes by setting the stage for the chapters to come. Mukesh Ambani's rise as a global business tycoon is a multifaceted tale of vision, determination, and calculated risk-taking. As the narrative unfolds, readers will witness how this business magnate navigated the complexities of geopolitics, technology, and finance to etch his name in the annals of global business history.

2

Architect of Progress: Mukesh Ambani's Leadership Philosophy

2.1 Visionary Leadership

Mukesh Ambani's meteoric rise as a global business tycoon is not merely a result of strategic business decisions; it is a testament to his distinctive leadership philosophy. This chapter begins by dissecting Ambani's leadership style, emphasizing the visionary mindset that sets him apart. From fostering innovation to cultivating a culture of excellence, Ambani's leadership is characterized by a forward-thinking approach that has propelled Reliance Industries to unparalleled heights.

2.2 Innovation at the Core

The heart of Ambani's leadership philosophy lies in a relentless pursuit of innovation. This section explores how Ambani fostered a culture of creativity and technological advancement within Reliance Industries. From the inception of groundbreaking projects to the development of cutting-edge technologies, Ambani's commitment to innovation permeates every facet of his leadership.

2.3 Balancing Tradition with Transformation

While innovation is a driving force, Ambani's leadership is also grounded in a deep respect for the traditional values instilled by his father, Dhirubhai Ambani. The chapter delves into how Mukesh seamlessly blended the old with the new, ensuring that Reliance Industries remained rooted in its heritage while embracing the winds of change. This delicate balance between tradition and transformation became a cornerstone of his leadership strategy.

2.4 People First: Building High-Performance Teams

An exploration of Mukesh Ambani's leadership philosophy would be incomplete without delving into his approach to human capital. This section examines Ambani's emphasis on nurturing talent, building high-performance teams, and fostering a culture of inclusivity within the organization. Through anecdotes and case studies, the chapter highlights the instrumental role of Reliance Industries' workforce in realizing Ambani's vision.

2.5 Risk-Taking and Resilience

A crucial aspect of Mukesh Ambani's leadership is his ability to take calculated risks. The chapter unfolds the stories of strategic decisions that defined his tenure, examining the risks involved and the resilience displayed in the face of challenges. Ambani's unwavering determination and capacity to navigate uncertainty emerge as key components of his leadership prowess.

2.6 Ethical Leadership in a Global Context

The chapter concludes by addressing the ethical dimensions of Ambani's leadership. It explores how he navigated the complex intersection of business and ethics, maintaining integrity in a rapidly evolving global business landscape. From corporate social responsibility initiatives to ethical business practices, Ambani's commitment to ethical leadership is a beacon for aspiring leaders worldwide.

As readers journey through Chapter 2, they will gain deeper insights into the qualities that distinguish Mukesh Ambani not only as a business magnate but as a leader whose philosophy transcends corporate boardrooms, leaving an indelible mark on the broader tapestry of global leadership.

3

Digital Dominion: Mukesh Ambani's Technological Triumph

3.1 The Digital Imperative

This chapter delves into Mukesh Ambani's strategic foray into the digital realm, positioning Reliance Industries as a major player in the tech landscape. It begins by chronicling the factors that led Ambani to recognize the digital imperative - the growing influence of technology, the rise of digital platforms, and the shifting dynamics of consumer behavior.

3.2 Jio: Revolutionizing Connectivity

At the heart of Ambani's digital strategy lies the revolutionary Jio project. The chapter explores the meticulous planning, infrastructure investments, and bold decisions that culminated in the launch of Jio. From providing affordable data services to transforming India into the world's largest consumer of mobile data, Jio's impact on the telecommunications landscape is dissected, showcasing Ambani's vision for a digitally connected nation.

3.3 E-Commerce Ambitions

As the narrative unfolds, attention shifts to Ambani's ambitious foray into the e-commerce sector. The strategic acquisitions, partnerships, and the launch of JioMart underscore his commitment to creating a seamless digital retail experience. This section explores how Ambani navigated the complexities of the e-commerce market, leveraging technology to integrate online and offline retail channels.

3.4 Future-Forward: Investments in Technology

Beyond telecommunications and e-commerce, Ambani's technological triumph extends to investments in cutting-edge technologies. From artificial intelligence to blockchain, this section unravels how Ambani positioned Reliance Industries at the forefront of technological innovation. The chapter examines key projects and collaborations that highlight Ambani's commitment to driving technological progress across various industries.

3.5 The Convergence Strategy

Mukesh Ambani's digital dominion is not confined to individual sectors; it involves a convergence strategy that integrates diverse businesses. The narrative unfolds how Ambani orchestrated the synergy between telecommunications, digital services, and traditional industries within the Reliance conglomerate. This convergence strategy, with technology as the linchpin, became a key driver of sustained growth and market dominance.

3.6 Global Aspirations: Beyond National Borders

The chapter concludes by exploring Mukesh Ambani's global aspirations in the digital realm. From international collaborations to expanding the footprint of Jio beyond India, this section illuminates Ambani's vision of positioning Reliance Industries as a global digital powerhouse. The challenges, triumphs, and strategic maneuvers on the global stage showcase Ambani's determination to transcend geographical boundaries in the digital domain.

Chapter 3 unravels the layers of Mukesh Ambani's technological triumph, revealing how he not only embraced the digital revolution but became a trailblazer, reshaping industries and economies through the strategic application of technology. As readers navigate through the digital landscape Ambani has carved, they witness a visionary leader harnessing the power of innovation to build a digital empire that extends beyond national borders.

4

Energy Metamorphosis: Mukesh Ambani's Sustainable Vision

4.1 Pioneering Sustainable Practices

This chapter delves into Mukesh Ambani's commitment to sustainable business practices and environmental stewardship. It begins by tracing the roots of this ethos within the Ambani family, exploring how Dhirubhai's legacy laid the groundwork for a corporate culture that values not only economic prosperity but also environmental responsibility.

4.2 Transformative Energy Ventures

As the narrative unfolds, attention shifts to Reliance Industries' ventures in the energy sector and Ambani's transformative initiatives. From green energy projects to investments in clean technologies, the chapter explores how Ambani navigated the evolving energy landscape, positioning Reliance as a pioneer in sustainable practices.

4.3 The Green Revolution: Ambani's Renewable Energy Pursuits

This section delves into Ambani's strategic investments in renewable energy, shedding light on the establishment of solar and wind energy projects. The chapter explores the challenges and successes in scaling up sustainable energy production, positioning Reliance Industries as a key player in the global shift towards cleaner, greener alternatives.

4.4 Circular Economy Initiatives

Ambani's commitment to sustainability extends beyond energy production to embrace a circular economy. This chapter examines how Reliance Industries implemented innovative recycling and waste management initiatives. Ambani's vision for a closed-loop system, minimizing environmental impact, is explored through the lens of specific projects and partnerships that exemplify his dedication to a sustainable future.

4.5 ESG Imperative: Embracing Environmental, Social, and Governance Values

A critical aspect of Ambani's sustainable vision is his emphasis on Environmental, Social, and Governance (ESG) values. The narrative explores how Reliance Industries aligns its business practices with these principles, addressing climate change, social responsibility, and corporate governance. The chapter outlines specific initiatives, policies, and partnerships that reflect Ambani's commitment to a holistic approach to sustainable business.

4.6 Global Leadership in Sustainability

The chapter concludes by positioning Mukesh Ambani as a global leader in sustainability. It highlights his efforts to drive conversations on environmental consciousness at international forums, collaborations with global organizations, and the influence of Reliance Industries in shaping sustainable practices beyond national borders. Ambani's role in advocating for a collective global effort towards sustainability is a testament to his vision extending far beyond business success.

Chapter 4 provides a comprehensive exploration of Mukesh Ambani's transformative approach to sustainability within the corporate landscape. As readers navigate through the chapters, they witness how Ambani's commitment to environmental responsibility has not only redefined Reliance Industries but has also positioned him as a trailblazer in fostering a sustainable and responsible future for businesses worldwide.

5

Navigating Challenges: Mukesh Ambani's Resilience in the Business Arena

5.1 The Nature of Challenges

This chapter opens by acknowledging the inevitability of challenges in the business arena and introduces readers to the various hurdles Mukesh Ambani encountered throughout his career. From economic downturns to industry disruptions, the narrative explores the nature of challenges that shaped Ambani's leadership journey.

5.2 Economic Downturns: Lessons from Adversity

The chapter delves into how Ambani navigated through economic downturns, examining the strategic decisions and risk-management strategies he employed to steer Reliance Industries through turbulent financial waters. Ambani's resilience and adaptability during challenging economic climates provide valuable lessons for aspiring entrepreneurs and business leaders.

5.3 Industry Disruptions: Adapting to Change

As industries underwent rapid transformations, Ambani faced the challenge of adapting to disruptive changes. This section explores how he identified emerging trends, embraced technological shifts, and positioned Reliance Industries to thrive in dynamic market landscapes. Case studies and anecdotes illustrate Ambani's ability to turn industry disruptions into opportunities for growth.

5.4 Regulatory Challenges: Navigating Legal and Regulatory Complexities

The narrative turns to the legal and regulatory challenges that Ambani encountered. From antitrust issues to compliance matters, this section explores how he navigated complex legal landscapes while upholding ethical standards. Ambani's strategic responses to regulatory challenges highlight his commitment to operating within legal frameworks while maintaining a competitive edge.

5.5 Global Geopolitical Shifts: Balancing International Dynamics

The chapter explores how Ambani's business empire faced challenges stemming from global geopolitical shifts. From trade tensions to diplomatic complexities, readers gain insights into Ambani's navigation through international dynamics. The narrative showcases his adeptness at balancing global forces while safeguarding the interests of Reliance Industries.

5.6 Crisis Leadership: The Reliance Response

The chapter concludes by examining Mukesh Ambani's crisis leadership during unprecedented events, such as the global pandemic. It explores how he steered Reliance Industries through times of crisis, emphasizing the resilience and agility required to weather unforeseen challenges. Case studies illustrate Ambani's crisis management strategies and the organizational resilience that defines his leadership legacy.

As readers journey through Chapter 5, they gain a profound understanding of Mukesh Ambani's ability to navigate and overcome challenges. Ambani's resilience in the face of adversity, strategic decision-making during economic downturns, and adaptability to industry disruptions provide valuable insights for business leaders, entrepreneurs, and students alike.

6

Legacy Beyond Profit: Mukesh Ambani's Philanthropy and Social Impact

6.1 The Philanthropic Imperative

This chapter delves into Mukesh Ambani's commitment to social responsibility and philanthropy, showcasing how his influence extends beyond boardrooms and into the broader fabric of society. The narrative begins by exploring the roots of Ambani's philanthropic values and the familial ethos that emphasizes giving back to the community.

6.2 Education Initiatives: Empowering Minds

A significant aspect of Ambani's philanthropy revolves around education initiatives. This section examines the establishment of educational institutions and scholarship programs, illustrating Ambani's belief in the transformative power of education. Case studies highlight the impact of these initiatives on individuals and communities, showcasing a commitment to empowering minds for a brighter future.

6.3 Healthcare: Nurturing Well-being

The chapter shifts focus to Ambani's contributions to the healthcare sector. From establishing medical facilities to supporting healthcare research, Ambani's philanthropy aims to improve healthcare access and outcomes. The narrative explores specific projects and collaborations that reflect his dedication to nurturing the well-being of communities.

6.4 Rural Development: Fostering Inclusive Growth

Ambani's philanthropic endeavors extend to rural development initiatives. This section explores how he has championed projects aimed at fostering inclusive growth in rural areas, addressing issues such as infrastructure, agriculture, and livelihoods. Case studies illuminate the tangible impact of these initiatives on the lives of individuals in rural communities.

6.5 Disaster Relief: Humanitarian Response

The narrative unfolds Ambani's humanitarian efforts in times of crisis, highlighting his rapid and effective responses to natural disasters and emergencies. From providing immediate relief to participating in long-term reconstruction efforts, Ambani's philanthropy extends to supporting communities during their most vulnerable moments.

6.6 The Ripple Effect: Beyond Charity

The chapter concludes by examining the broader societal impact of Ambani's philanthropy. It explores how his commitment to social responsibility has influenced other corporations, inspiring a culture of giving within the business community. The ripple effect of Ambani's philanthropy extends beyond individual projects, shaping a broader narrative of corporate social responsibility in India and beyond.

Chapter 6 provides a comprehensive exploration of Mukesh Ambani's philanthropic endeavors and social impact. As readers navigate through the chapter, they witness how Ambani's commitment to making a positive difference in society aligns with his business success, creating a legacy that extends far beyond profit margins and business achievements.

7

Future Horizons: Mukesh Ambani's Vision for Tomorrow

7.1 Anticipating Future Trends

This chapter delves into Mukesh Ambani's forward-looking vision for the future. It begins by exploring his ability to anticipate and leverage emerging trends, positioning Reliance Industries at the forefront of industries poised for growth.

7.2 Technology and Innovation Roadmap

The narrative unfolds Ambani's roadmap for technology and innovation, offering insights into the investments, research, and partnerships that define his strategy. From advancements in artificial intelligence to the integration of cutting-edge technologies, readers gain a glimpse into how Ambani envisions technology shaping the future landscape of business.

7.3 Sustainable Business Practices: A Long-Term Commitment

Ambani's commitment to sustainability extends beyond the present, shaping a vision for a future where businesses play a pivotal role in addressing environmental challenges. The chapter explores his strategies for embedding sustainability into the core of business operations, envisioning a future where corporations actively contribute to a more sustainable planet.

7.4 Global Expansion: Building on International Success

The narrative shifts to Ambani's aspirations for global expansion. From consolidating Reliance Industries' presence in international markets to venturing into new territories, this section explores how Ambani envisions the globalization of his business empire and the challenges and opportunities that lie on the path to international success.

7.5 Technological Convergence: Breaking Industry Silos

A key element of Ambani's future vision involves the convergence of technologies across industries. This section explores how he aims to break traditional industry silos, fostering a seamless integration of technologies to drive innovation and efficiency on a global scale.

7.6 Beyond Business: Socioeconomic Impact

The chapter concludes by highlighting Ambani's vision for the broader socioeconomic impact of his business ventures. From job creation to community development, readers gain insights into how Ambani envisions a future where the success of Reliance Industries contributes not only to economic prosperity but also to societal well-being.

As readers navigate through Chapter 7, they gain a deep understanding of Mukesh Ambani's futuristic vision. His anticipation of trends, commitment to technological advancement, and focus on sustainability collectively paint a picture of a leader who not only adapts to the future but actively shapes it, leaving an indelible mark on the global business landscape.

8

Mukesh Ambani's Leadership Lessons: Insights for Aspiring Entrepreneurs

8.1 The Leadership Tapestry

This chapter distills the essence of Mukesh Ambani's leadership journey, weaving together the threads of vision, resilience, innovation, and social responsibility. It sets the stage by reflecting on the leadership tapestry that has defined Ambani's trajectory in the business world.

8.2 Visionary Leadership: Looking Beyond Horizons

The narrative unfolds key lessons on visionary leadership, emphasizing the importance of looking beyond immediate challenges and envisioning the long-term impact of business decisions. Ambani's ability to anticipate trends and position Reliance Industries as a global player serves as a beacon for aspiring entrepreneurs with bold aspirations.

8.3 Resilience in the Face of Challenges

The chapter explores Ambani's resilience as a cornerstone of his leadership philosophy. From economic downturns to industry disruptions, readers gain insights into the mindset and strategies that have allowed Ambani to navigate challenges with fortitude and emerge stronger.

8.4 Innovation as a Catalyst for Success

Innovation is dissected as a driving force behind Ambani's success. The chapter explores how he nurtures a culture of creativity within his organizations, fostering an environment where innovation becomes a catalyst for growth and a means to stay ahead in a rapidly evolving business landscape.

8.5 People-Centric Leadership: Building High-Performance Teams

Ambani's emphasis on people-centric leadership is highlighted, offering lessons on building and leading high-performance teams. From talent acquisition to fostering a culture of inclusivity, readers gain insights into how Ambani leverages human capital as a strategic asset.

8.6 Ethical Leadership in a Global Context

The chapter delves into Ambani's commitment to ethical leadership, exploring lessons on navigating the complex intersection of business and ethics. From corporate social responsibility to upholding integrity in the face of challenges, Ambani's ethical approach serves as a guide for aspiring leaders in a global context.

8.7 Balancing Tradition with Transformation

The narrative reflects on Ambani's skillful balance between tradition and transformation, offering lessons on how leaders can draw inspiration from the past while adapting to the demands of the present and future. The chapter explores the value of heritage in shaping a sustainable and culturally rooted business strategy.

8.8 A Philanthropic Legacy: Lessons in Social Responsibility

The chapter concludes by distilling lessons from Ambani's philanthropic endeavors, emphasizing the importance of incorporating social responsibility into business strategies. Ambani's legacy of giving back to the community serves as a powerful lesson for aspiring entrepreneurs seeking to make a positive impact beyond profit margins.

Chapter 8 serves as a compendium of leadership lessons drawn from Mukesh Ambani's remarkable journey. As readers reflect on these insights, they gain valuable perspectives that transcend industries and borders, offering a roadmap for aspiring entrepreneurs and business leaders aiming to make a lasting mark on the global stage.

9

Mukesh Ambani's Enduring Legacy: Shaping the Future Landscape

9.1 The Evolution of Ambani's Legacy

This chapter embarks on a reflective journey, tracing the evolution of Mukesh Ambani's legacy from its inception to the present day. It explores how his impact has rippled through the business world, leaving an indelible mark on industries, communities, and the global perception of Indian entrepreneurship.

9.2 The Reliance Ecosystem: Symbiosis of Industries

The narrative delves into the interconnectedness of industries within the Reliance ecosystem, showcasing how Ambani's strategic vision has created a symbiotic relationship among diverse sectors. From energy to telecommunications, readers gain insights into the seamless integration that defines the Reliance conglomerate.

9.3 Global Recognition: Ambani as a Business Icon

The chapter explores Mukesh Ambani's standing on the global stage, examining the accolades and recognition he has received as a business icon. From influential lists to international forums, Ambani's presence has transcended national boundaries, contributing to a positive perception of Indian entrepreneurship worldwide.

9.4 The Next Generation: Ambani's Legacy in Succession

A critical aspect of Ambani's legacy is the transition to the next generation. The chapter reflects on the succession plan within the Ambani family, exploring how the principles and values instilled by Mukesh Ambani are being carried forward by the next generation of leaders within the Reliance conglomerate.

9.5 Continued Innovation: A Legacy of Progress

The narrative unfolds how Ambani's legacy is not static but continues to evolve through ongoing innovation. From technological advancements to novel business ventures, readers gain insights into how Ambani's vision for progress remains a driving force shaping the future landscape.

9.6 The Humanitarian Impact: Beyond Business

Ambani's legacy extends beyond business success to encompass a significant humanitarian impact. This section explores the lasting effects of his philanthropy and social responsibility initiatives, showcasing how they have contributed to positive societal change.

9.7 Lessons for Future Leaders

The chapter concludes by distilling the overarching lessons from Ambani's enduring legacy. It reflects on how future leaders can draw inspiration from his journey, applying the principles of visionary leadership, resilience, innovation, and social responsibility to navigate the challenges and opportunities that lie ahead.

Chapter 9 serves as a retrospective on Mukesh Ambani's enduring legacy, encapsulating the multifaceted impact of his leadership on businesses, industries, and society at large. As readers reflect on the final chapter, they gain a comprehensive understanding of how Ambani's influence will continue to shape the future landscape of global business and philanthropy.

10

Reflections on Mukesh Ambani's Impact: A Global Perspective

10.1 The Global Business Landscape

This concluding chapter takes a step back to reflect on Mukesh Ambani's impact within the broader context of the global business landscape. It examines the trends, shifts, and challenges shaping industries worldwide and contextualizes Ambani's influence within this dynamic environment.

10.2 Ambani's Global Legacy

The narrative explores how Mukesh Ambani's legacy extends far beyond national borders, influencing not only Indian business but also contributing to the global narrative of entrepreneurship. It reflects on his role as a global business leader and the lessons that leaders around the world can draw from his journey.

10.3 Global Collaborations and Partnerships

The chapter delves into Ambani's strategic collaborations and partnerships on the international stage. From alliances with global tech giants to cross-border investments, readers gain insights into how Ambani has fostered relationships that transcend geographical boundaries, contributing to a more interconnected global business ecosystem.

10.4 The Technological Wave: Global Implications

Ambani's impact on the technological landscape is explored in the context of global implications. The narrative reflects on how his ventures, particularly in telecommunications and digital technologies, have set the stage for global discussions on connectivity, innovation, and the role of technology in shaping economies.

10.5 Lessons for Global Leaders

The chapter distills universal lessons from Mukesh Ambani's leadership journey. It reflects on how leaders across diverse industries and regions can apply Ambani's principles of visionary leadership, resilience, innovation, and social responsibility to navigate the complexities of the global business arena.

10.6 Future Trajectories: Global Business Trends

The narrative concludes by contemplating the potential trajectories of global business trends and how Ambani's impact might shape or respond to these changes. It invites readers to ponder the evolving nature of industries, the influence of technology, and the role of responsible business practices in shaping the future.

10.7 Ambani's Enduring Presence

The final chapter closes by acknowledging the enduring presence of Mukesh

Ambani's influence. It reflects on how his legacy will continue to reverberate through the corridors of business, technology, and philanthropy, leaving an imprint on the global stage for generations to come.

Chapter 10 serves as a reflective conclusion to the exploration of Mukesh Ambani's impact. As readers consider the global implications of his leadership, they gain a panoramic view of how Ambani's journey contributes to the broader narrative of business leadership in a rapidly evolving world.

11

Mukesh Ambani's Continued Journey: Navigating New Frontiers

11.1 The Ever-Evolving Vision

This chapter opens by examining Mukesh Ambani's ongoing journey, highlighting how his vision continues to evolve in response to the dynamic nature of the business landscape. It explores the latest ventures, strategic shifts, and emerging priorities that characterize the current phase of Ambani's leadership.

11.2 New Horizons in Technology

The narrative unfolds the latest advancements and forays into technology, illustrating how Ambani is navigating the ever-changing tech landscape. From exploring emerging technologies to the integration of artificial intelligence, readers gain insights into how Ambani is positioning Reliance Industries at the forefront of technological innovation.

11.3 Global Expansion Strategies

The chapter delves into Ambani's strategies for global expansion in the present context. It explores recent international collaborations, acquisitions, and market entries, shedding light on how Reliance Industries is expanding its footprint and influence on the global stage.

11.4 Sustainability in the Modern Context

Building on Ambani's commitment to sustainability, this section examines how current initiatives are addressing contemporary environmental challenges. It explores new projects, partnerships, and innovative approaches that reflect Ambani's dedication to shaping a more sustainable and responsible future.

11.5 The Next Generation's Role

As Ambani's legacy is poised for continuity through the next generation, this section reflects on the evolving roles and contributions of the Ambani family members within the leadership structure of Reliance Industries. It explores how the transition is unfolding and the strategic directions pursued by the upcoming leaders.

11.6 Lessons from the Recent Past

Reflecting on recent challenges and triumphs, this part of the chapter distills lessons from Ambani's leadership in the face of contemporary economic, technological, and geopolitical shifts. It offers insights into how Ambani's approach to leadership is adapting to meet the demands of the current business landscape.

11.7 Ambani's Place in Business History

The chapter concludes by contemplating Mukesh Ambani's place in the annals of business history. It reflects on his enduring impact, contributions to global business, and the legacy that he is shaping in real-time. The narrative invites readers to consider the potential future chapters in Ambani's story and the mark he will leave on business history.

Chapter 11 serves as a snapshot of Mukesh Ambani's continued journey, providing readers with a current perspective on his leadership, strategies, and the evolving legacy of Reliance Industries. As the narrative unfolds, readers gain a sense of the ongoing narrative in Ambani's storied career and the exciting frontiers that lie ahead.

12

Mukesh Ambani's Enduring Impact: A Legacy of Leadership

12.1 A Reflective Journey

This concluding chapter serves as a reflective culmination of Mukesh Ambani's enduring impact. It invites readers to journey back through the narrative, revisiting key milestones, lessons, and insights gleaned from Ambani's life and leadership journey.

12.2 The Evergreen Principles

The chapter distills the timeless principles embedded in Ambani's leadership philosophy. It reflects on the enduring nature of visionary thinking, resilience, innovation, ethical leadership, and social responsibility—principles that transcend specific industries and time periods.

12.3 The Reliance Legacy

As readers reflect on Ambani's legacy, the narrative turns to the lasting impact of the Reliance conglomerate. It explores how Reliance Industries, under Ambani's leadership, has not only shaped industries but has also played a transformative role in the economic and social fabric of the regions it operates in.

12.4 Lessons for Future Generations

Building on the lessons drawn throughout the narrative, this section distills guidance for future generations of leaders. It encourages aspiring entrepreneurs and business leaders to draw inspiration from Ambani's journey, emphasizing the importance of vision, resilience, innovation, ethical leadership, and social impact.

12.5 Ambani's Impact on Global Business

The chapter expands its focus to the global impact of Mukesh Ambani's leadership. It reflects on how his influence has contributed to reshaping the perception of Indian business globally and the role he has played in discussions on technology, sustainability, and corporate social responsibility on the world stage.

12.6 The Continuing Journey

While encapsulating Ambani's enduring impact, this section acknowledges that the journey is ongoing. It contemplates the potential trajectories and contributions that may unfold in the next chapters of Mukesh Ambani's career, recognizing that his influence is far from reaching its culmination.

12.7 Ambani's Invitation to the Future

The narrative concludes by extending an invitation to the future. It invites readers to witness, participate, and contribute to the unfolding legacy of Mukesh Ambani—a legacy that continues to shape the contours of business, technology, and philanthropy on a global scale.

Chapter 12 serves as a reflective epilogue, encapsulating the enduring impact of Mukesh Ambani's leadership journey. As readers close this final chapter, they carry with them the wisdom, insights, and inspiration drawn from Ambani's story—a story that continues to be written on the canvas of global business and leadership.

13

Summary

In this comprehensive exploration of Mukesh Ambani's life and career, the narrative unfolds across twelve chapters, tracing his journey from the early days in the Ambani family to his current position as a global business icon. The chapters delve into various aspects of Ambani's leadership, including his visionary approach, innovative strategies, commitment to sustainability, and philanthropic initiatives.

Chapter 1: "A Vision Takes Root"
   - Introduces Ambani's early life, family legacy, and educational background.
   - Highlights his foray into the business world, taking over the reins of Reliance Industries.

Chapter 2: "Architect of Progress: Mukesh Ambani's Leadership Philosophy"
   - Explores Ambani's distinctive leadership style, emphasizing innovation, balance, and a people-centric approach.

Chapter 3: "Digital Dominion: Mukesh Ambani's Technological Triumph"
   - Chronicles Ambani's transformative impact on the telecommunications and digital industries with the launch of Jio.
   - Examines his forays into e-commerce, global technology investments, and the convergence of digital services.

Chapter 4: "Energy Metamorphosis: Mukesh Ambani's Sustainable Vision"
   - Details Ambani's commitment to sustainable business practices, including renewable energy initiatives and circular economy projects.

Chapter 5: "Navigating Challenges: Mukesh Ambani's Resilience in the Business Arena"
   - Explores Ambani's response to economic downturns, industry disruptions, regulatory challenges, and global geopolitical shifts.

Chapter 6: "Legacy Beyond Profit: Mukesh Ambani's Philanthropy and Social Impact"
   - Examines Ambani's philanthropic initiatives, including education, healthcare, rural development, and disaster relief.

Chapter 7: "Future Horizons: Mukesh Ambani's Vision for Tomorrow"
   - Explores Ambani's forward-looking vision, including technology and innovation roadmaps, global expansion strategies, and sustainability goals.

Chapter 8: "Mukesh Ambani's Leadership Lessons: Insights for Aspiring Entrepreneurs"
   - Distills leadership lessons from Ambani's journey, including visionary thinking, resilience, innovation, and ethical leadership.

Chapter 9: "Mukesh Ambani's Enduring Legacy: Shaping the Future Landscape"
   - Reflects on the evolution of Ambani's legacy, including the interconnected Reliance ecosystem, global recognition, and the role of the next generation.

Chapter 10: "Reflections on Mukesh Ambani's Impact: A Global Perspective"
   - Reflects on Ambani's impact within the global business landscape, exploring collaborations, technological implications, and lessons for global leaders.

SUMMARY

Chapter 11: "Mukesh Ambani's Continued Journey: Navigating New Frontiers"
 - Explores Ambani's ongoing ventures, including technological advancements, global expansion, sustainability initiatives, and the roles of the next generation.

Chapter 12: "Mukesh Ambani's Enduring Impact: A Legacy of Leadership"
 - Concludes with a reflective summary of Ambani's impact, distilling timeless principles, acknowledging his influence on global business, and extending an invitation to the future.

This comprehensive exploration provides readers with a multifaceted understanding of Mukesh Ambani's life, leadership, and lasting impact on the global business landscape.

www.ingramcontent.com/pod-product-compliance
Lightning Source LLC
LaVergne TN
LVHW020739090526
838202LV00057BA/5988